THIS IS WHAT HAPPENED
IN OUR OTHER LIFE

ACHY OBEJAS

BODY LANGUAGE 01

A MIDSUMMER NIGHT'S PRESS

New York

for Cathy

Cover photograph © Ruth Thorne-Thomsen:
Chair over Point, WI, 1983
courtesy Catherine Edelman Gallery, Chicago.

A Midsummer Night's Press
16 West 36th Street
2nd Floor
New York, NY 10018
amidsummernightspress@gmail.com
www.amidsummernightspress.com

Grateful acknowledgments are made to the magazines
and anthologies where some of these poems,
sometimes in earlier versions, first appeared:
*The Antigosh Review, Ecos, Helicon Nine, Phoebe,
QRHYME, Rambunctious Review, Samisdat,
Strong Coffee,* and *The World in Us* (St. Martin's Press).

Designed by Marróndediseño *www.quintatinta.com.*

First edition, November 2007.

ISBN-13: 978-0-9794208-2-5
ISBN-10: 0-9794208-2-2

Printed in Spain.
Depósito legal: M-44537-2007

CONTENTS

LEGACIES

The first time I was inside a woman,
I was confused.
I didn't recognize her, or myself.
I thought I was swimming, but in air.
Maybe flying, underwater.

There are secrets only the body yields,
like vibration,
and kissing, a happy accident
between two women
who have already exhausted all words.

BY THE SIDE OF THE ROAD
THIS SUMMER

Let me love this, the fine turn of your ankle,
gym shoes on the fence and sand everywhere; a nest.
You turn so fine, special film, easy motion.

You turn out to be
a runner, perfect swimmer,
warm mammal hissing slow through the weeds.

"I've got a handful of you," you say,
thumping your chest, tough heart.
You're this size.

In the meantime, your T-shirt, wet and bright,
flap flaps like a telegraph on my skin
these painful pleasures.

MOUNT NEBO

This is what happened in our other life:
we stared at the grit at the bottom of the cup,
a sorcerer's Rorschach that guaranteed felicity,
and we drank it, bitterness and all,
because in that other life –
the one in which we talked back to god,
convinced god to let us have both milk and honey in our cup
(the milk of our bodies, buttery kisses,
honeycomb caves perfected by stingerless bees) –
there is no pain, you see, no pain.
There is only fullness there.

I can see, I can see it from here.

THE COLLECTION

Your promise is the rose petal on the sill
remembering the garden.

I turn it, like a tried ignition,
and catch something else:
a window fog, clear sadness.
A tear, moist on your lip.

It's winter and your coat squeaks.
I find you under the layers,
stiff as a nun, warm.

Now I will tell you about my promise,
how I keep the petals
with philatelic precision.

DANCING IN PARADISE

You lean against me
as we dance, the soft huddle
of our heads together,
our breaths clean steam in the blue
smoke, rapid, exhausted.
We mix margaritas, because
I like the name, a
woman you love. You're older.
I'm willing, drunk, unbuttoned.
You lead, peeling layer after
wet layer, a heap
of sweaters, shirts and precious
metals. Your breast is
slick with sweat, hands agile,
eels in glass waters.
When you scoop me up, I twist
in your lap, a thick
needle thrust through my tongue. Later,
you give me a reading list,
blank journals, your mother's

recipes. You take
what you need, knowing there's no
autonomy of the
senses, those five carnivores
in their own essential
food chain. What survives is memory,
twin jewels, the blade of
a pelvic bone. Instinctively,
we keep our eyes open,
ears keen, for marine smells,
salt, the plexus of light,
sound, water.

IN THE AFTERNOON

You worry between the pots and pans
about your body swollen;
straightening your back,
the snail's roundness your own.
You cringe. You're embarrassed.
You see too many similarities with the soup spoons.
"It's nothing," you say,
your skin rice paper, tea color,
and musty like a morning bed.

In the afternoon, we buy bread
and cheese, hard because
you want to cut it with a blade.
Your finger has string around it
to remind you of me.
You add wine to the shopping list.

I want to take two hours to read,
to do nothing, to find a place on the tree
to carve our initials. I have no knife.

You, stretching, reach for the ceiling
and blue lines shoot through
the inside of your arm – neon,
a boulevard, water for the garden.
You laugh, tell me I would not survive
in the wet, black-green of the forest.
"Your skin," you say, touching this, touching that,
"is too light, too bright. Something would eat you."

I want to take a long nap,
stiff-fingered, limp breasts,
sour-sweet like a baby's breath,
in the cave, in the cave.

MONDAY IN APRIL

All your lovers come to you in April,
or you to them.
Spring offerings, rain and rhododendron.
Later, the smell of smoke.

You are tugging on my hair, a playful threat.
You find a spot below my neck, near the spine,
and spread flat the palm of your hand
like sealing wax, or a rheostat.
This is familiar, like a postcard
from the old country, the mother country,
with its distant safety, its sunny skies
always a shade of blue.
Intimate and exotic, the lights askew,
a rhomboid map.

In the car, I am following all the signs,
my feet taking turns, dancing.
(I would get rid of the car.)
This is Illinois, Chicago, dead industry,

the car like an iron lung.

Now everything is concrete. The white lines,
the curb, the porter at the airport,
the catch growing in my throat.

THE DARKNESS

I wasn't looking for anything, not me,
dancing there in the darkness,
swinging my arms up like that,
my hands folded into fists
that pummeled the shocking
lights from the stage.

It's not that I wanted
to dance, no.
I wanted a way to disguise
my disgust,
to exhaust the anger
that threatened to burn
with thick black smoke.
I wanted to hit something
– anything –
hurt no one.

"Okay," you say, "but
that passed already.

It's morning."
You pour hot water
over a tea bag and
tell me my hair's standing on end.
Light streams in through the blinds,
lines and lines of it, spilling
over me, then you.

You rub my head, my stomach,
first with the heel of your hand,
then with your fingers. I'm
thinking of factories, of panes
of glass thick with dirt,
and of hunger.

I want a spring that runs
into another spring,
a choking rain forest,
stones grafted onto one another
by layers and layers of fossils.

LOVE

it is like a small pain
insignificant

at first you don't notice it at all

(later, when it heals
the absence will hurt
more than the pain itself)

it is never just one hundred percent
cotton for cuddling; the smell of sleep;
delicious cold coffee; sunday mornings
marked with shy letters on the calendar;
the new york times in disarray; easy
conspiratorial silences; the mischievous
secret in public places; a tug on
the shoulders by suddenly little
fingers ...

never just the intimate sounds of

breathing; the familiar names;
the secure tones and
modulations; even the contrary habits that
become endearing

there comes a point
when you accept the pain
like daily bread
a nutritional catalyst

the barometer

THE HABITS OF THE BLIND

I am staring at a grey, pink and purple sky,
worrying about the imprint of our first embrace
(that awkward tangle of limbs),
the first time we were skin on skin.
What will sustain us later,
when we know everything,
if not this innocence?
I worry too much, and not enough.
I long ago surrendered:
The world breaks us all,
throws us up against the wall,
splits our hearts with a vengeance.
There is no right person.
We will love the wrong people.
What I've done is this: embraced chaos –
studied the habits of the blind,
their sixth sense, and Braille.
This way, I've learned to read my lovers' scars,
to appreciate the force or cunning
behind each cut,

the meanings of each tender pattern,
the beauty, and depth.
Pain is the risk and the measure
not just of how far we're willing to go,
but of how much we're willing to feel
later, alone in the dark.

SLEEPING APART

This night stalker, the
bastard –
wounds, primordial
as a fetal crouch,
punctured;
my solar plexus,
a scoop of air.

The nightmare is itself
the somnambulist, time-zone
zombie unaware,
bumping
the furniture, telephone,
eating its own tail.

This lover – me –
I can't dream, can't sleep,
can't will away this heartache.

Here, then, each membrane
plays systole dances;
all else
is Morse codes, satellites –
greater and greater distance.

SUNDAY

Love set them going, our mothers,
tiny little wind-up toys
as shiny and urgent as pearls;
later dull and slow, like late model cars,
something bloated about their design.

Love set them going, directed
their noses to the clean cosmetic,
the innocent films.
They married one man;
they made love only once.

It was love that gave them careers,
new wares, made them
dark-haired girls sifting rice,
checking magazines for quick tests titled:
"Do you know your lover?"
"Is your marriage happy?"
Everyday the air of nitrous oxide.

They never told the fathers about us,
the daughters standing with arms akimbo.
We were the open secret,
as beautiful and repellent as tattoos.

Now they see themselves the snail on the tank.
We are stone nymphs come to life,
brilliant betas,
too many things at once.

I tell you, if you whisper to me, woman,
it goes no further.
Pain or peace, I cannot take it to them.
If you touch me, your albuminous kiss,
that is between you and me.

It is love, casuist love, a twisted Gabriel
who turns them away:
Our mothers, black veils, votive, orthodox,
gravely whispering to men
misdemeanor sins.

They light dripless, traceless,
invisible candles for penance,
sing prayers like insurance,
dream crashes in station wagons, family cars.

Year after year, the missal for breakfast.

When we become them, a little taller perhaps,
buddha women late in life,
will we be like them,
with our steeples and postulates,
trembling?

Tell me, here, with a tremor of a different sort,
our eyes lidless, your breath cool,
about our mortality.

GOODBY

Every detail is an accident,
the horror
of the next moment.
You will peel from me like
plastic surgery;
later a tuck, a fold.
Public appearances matter so.

There is nothing in this book
but white pages,
empty with colors,
abstract mathematics.
In the margins, I hold on
to simply functions.

Breakfast.
Blueberries and cream,
almost acid.
Snakes at the supermarket.
The ink from the tabloids

unraveling.

When you come to pick up your letters –
your shadow two embarrassed men
from the moving company –
I will scatter the ashes.

TRANSITION

The phone is still warm to the touch
as I wander from room to room, salt in my coffee …
My fingers will not dial again, will not enter you,
will not tap casually in the aftermath.
Instead, I will drink the coffee, briny in my mouth.
I will not listen for the dial tone, for the bells, for the
                cautious rise
in your voice, for the brightening when you first hear me,
                for the
sound of your laughter in the cathedral floating toward the
                heavens
with the unthinking certainty of the faithful. I will pretend
I don't believe. You would remind me that you accept
the mystery of death as a matter of cold-hard fact, that you
can only consider the here and now, that you can't
                anticipate
the next hour, much less the possibility of what …
That we … ? That *we* … ?
I put the coffee down unsteadily, watch the cup fall and
                split.

You keep your back to the phone, your index finger
(in Spanish, god's finger) intent on new stories, revisions,
oblivion. I pick up the phone. You turn on your computer.
I turn the receiver in my hand, admiring its contour, its
                weight.
You check your correspondence and the world on the screen
is everything. I fold my fist around the receiver like a black
                jack,
smack it into my open palm, then my knuckles.
And *this* is everything.

HISTORIA DE AMOR

Ella no existía
cuando la otra se fue.
Después, no se enteró de su regreso.
Se vieron de casualidad.
Una cruzaba la calle,
la otra esperaba un carro.
Se imaginaron un beso
(más bien un roce de labios,
la mano en el vientre).
Siguieron
cada una por su camino.
Una miró hacia atrás.
La otra no.

ACHY OBEJAS (Havana, 1956) is the author of two novels, *Days of Awe* (Ballantine) and *Memory Mambo* (Cleis), both of which won the Lambda Literary Award, as well as the short story collection *We Came All the Way From Cuba so You Could Dress Like This?* (Cleis). She is also editor of the anthology *Havana Noir* (Akashic).

Her poetry has appeared in numerous journals, including *Conditions, The Antigosh Review, Helcion Nine, Phoebe, Revista Chicano-Rique,* and *The Beloit Poetry Journal,* and she received an NEA Fellowship in Poetry in 1986.

An accomplished journalist, she worked at the *Chicago Tribune* for more than a decade, and has also written for the *Village Voice,* the *Los Angeles Times, Vogue, Playboy, Ms., The Nation, The Advocate, Windy City Times, High Performance, Chicago Sun-Times, Chicago Reader, Nerve.com, Latina,* and the *Washington Post,* among others.

Among her many honors, she has received a Pulitzer for a *Tribune* team investigation, the Studs Terkel Journalism Prize, and several Peter Lisagor journalism honors, as well as residencies at Yaddo, Ragdale, and the Virginia Center for the Arts.

She has served as Springer Writer-in-Residence at the University of Chicago and the Distinguished Writer in Residence at the University of Hawai'i, and is currently the Sor Juana Visiting Writer at DePaul University in Chicago.

A MIDSUMMER NIGHT'S PRESS was founded by Lawrence Schimel in New Haven, CT in 1991. Using a letterpress, it published broadsides of poems by Nancy Willard, Joe Haldeman, and Jane Yolen, among others, in signed, limited editions of 126 copies, numbered 1–100 and lettered A–Z. One of the broadsides—"Will" by Jane Yolen—won a Rhysling Award. In 1993, the publisher moved to New York and the press went on hiatus until 2007, when it began publishing perfect-bound, commercially-printed chapbooks under three imprints:

FABULA RASA: devoted to works inspired by mythology, folklore, and fairy tales. The first title from this imprint is *Fairy Tales for Writers* by Lawrence Schimel.

FUNNY BONES: devoted to works of humor and light verse. The first titles from this imprint are *The Good-Neighbor Policy,* a murder mystery told in double dactyls by Edgar Award-winner Charles Ardai, and *Irreverent Biographies*, an anthology of clerihews.

BODY LANGUAGE: devoted to texts exploring questions of gender and sexual identity. The first titles from this imprint are *This Is What Happened in Our Other Life* by Achy Obejas and the new annual anthologies *Best Gay Poetry* and *Best Lesbian Poetry*.